21st
Century
Junior
Library

WORKING AT THE LIBRARY

by Katie Marsico

CHERRY LAKE PUBLISHING * ANN ARBOR, MICHIGAN

Published in the United States of America by Cherry Lake Publishing
Ann Arbor, Michigan
www.cherrylakepublishing.com

Content Adviser: Olivia Nellums, Reference and Instruction Librarian, Camden County College
Reading Adviser: Cecilia Minden-Cupp, PhD, Literacy Consultant

Page 4, ©iStockphoto.com/wsphotos; page 6, ©Terrie L. Zeller, used under license from Shutterstock, Inc.; page 8, ©iStockphoto.com/lisafx; cover and page 10, ©iStockphoto.com/Jbryson; page 12, ©iStockphoto.com/acilo; cover and page 14, ©iStockphoto.com/nano; page 16, ©michaeljung, used under license from Shutterstock, Inc.; cover and page 18, ©Publicimage/Dreamstime.com; cover and page 20, ©Rob Marmion, used under license from Shutterstock, Inc.

LIBRARY OF CONGRESS CATALOGING-IN-PUBLICATION DATA
Marsico, Katie, 1980–
  Working at the library / by Katie Marsico.
     p. cm.—(21st century junior library)
Includes index.
ISBN-13: 978-1-60279-511-2
ISBN-10: 1-60279-511-8
1. Libraries—Juvenile literature. 2. Librarians—Juvenile literature.
I. Title. II. Series.
Z665.5.M36 2010
027—dc22   2008046010

Cherry Lake Publishing would like to acknowledge the work of
The Partnership for 21st Century Skills.
Please visit www.21stcenturyskills.org for more information.

CONTENTS

You can find books about almost any subject
at the library.

What Is a Library?

You look from side to side as you wander past shelves of books. You need books about airplanes for a school report. Aha! You finally find the ones you wanted to read. Now you must check these books out. Where are you? You are at the library.

People can use headphones when working on computers at some libraries.

Some people **borrow** books at the library. Others use the computers there. Many people just want a quiet spot to study. The library is a place to read and learn new things.

Create!

Draw a picture of your library. Show all your favorite areas. Be sure to draw all the workers. You may discover that more people work at a library than you thought!

Library workers like answering questions and helping people.

Who do you ask if you want to use a library computer? Where can you find your favorite book? Library workers are happy to help! They want you to enjoy a quiet place where you can learn and read. Are you ready to learn about library helpers?

Many librarians enjoy sharing books
with children.

Library Workers

Librarians do many jobs. Some help people find books. Others help students who are working on school projects. Some librarians spend all of their time with children. They read stories to kids just like you. All of them want you to enjoy visiting the library.

Who is this librarian talking to? She might be answering a question for a student working on a project.

It is easy to have fun at the library. You can look at many interesting books. Librarians make sure the library has many different books for you to read. They order books that they think you will like.

Look!

Look around. Libraries have many things besides books for you to enjoy. Can you name other items that you borrow or use? Here's a hint: two examples are magazines and CDs.

Clerks use special machines to check library items in and out.

Who helps you when it's time to check out a book? **Clerks** help you borrow items from the library. They also check in any items that you return.

You need a **library card** to check out books. How can you get a library card? A clerk can help you sign up for your own card.

Shelvers make sure library shelves look neat
and organized.

Some library workers work with computers more than books. They can answer questions about using the library's computers.

Who else works at the library? **Shelvers** are workers who **sort** through books. They put items in the right spot on library shelves.

A **custodian** is another library worker. He keeps the library clean.

The library needs many helpers. They all want you to have fun learning!

Most library workers will be happy to answer
questions about their jobs.

Do You Want to Work at a Library?

Would you like to work at a library someday? Start planning now. Pay attention to all the workers you see at the library. Talk to them. Try to find out more about the jobs they do.

You might discover that most library workers enjoy reading. Many like helping you think about new ideas.

Do you like helping people find answers? Think about working in a library!

How can you prepare for a job at the library? Become a good reader who loves books. You should also be good at using computers.

Libraries are exciting places to work. Find out as much as you can now. This will help you decide if a library job is right for you!

Ask Questions!

Are you planning to visit the library? Think of questions to ask library workers. Ask the librarian what he likes best about his work. Ask the clerk how she chose this job. Asking questions helps you learn more about jobs that interest you.

GLOSSARY

borrow (BAR-oh) to take something that you plan to return later

clerks (KLURKS) library workers who do many tasks such as checking items in and out

custodian (kuhs-TOH-dee-uhn) a worker who cleans the library

librarians (lye-BRER-ee-uhnz) workers who have many jobs at the library such as helping people find books

library card (LYE-brer-ee KARD) a special card you can use to check out items from the library

shelvers (SHELV-urz) workers who place books and other items on the library's shelves

sort (SORT) to separate or put things in a certain order

FIND OUT MORE

BOOKS

Jango-Cohen, Judith. *Librarians.* Minneapolis: Lerner Publications Co., 2005.

Sweeney, Alyse. *Welcome to the Library.* New York: Children's Press, 2007.

WEB SITES

PBS Kids—Play-Maker: D.W. Gets Her Library Card
pbskids.org/arthur/print/playmaker/script/
Read a fun script and act out a play about the items a library has to offer

U.S. Department of Labor—Bureau of Labor Statistics (Librarian)
www.bls.gov/k12/reading04.htm
Learn more about being a librarian and how you can prepare for this job

INDEX

ABOUT THE AUTHOR

Katie Marsico is the author of more than 50 children's books. She lives in Elmhurst, Illinois, with her husband and children. She would especially like to thank Karen Pepple of the Elmhurst Public Library for helping her research this title.

ML   S/11